Be Your Own *Pet*
Therapist

*Energy Based Recipes for Positive **Pet**
Behavior and Health*

By Susan Wright, Ph.D.

Creative Life Change Books
2005

Library of Congress Card Number: TXu1-192-150

ISBN: 0-9763204-0-1

Book design & photography by Layla Wingate
San Rafael, California
www.laylawingate.com

Published by Creative Life Change Books
Corte Madera, California
www.advicelink.com

Printed in China

First Edition

Disclaimer:

This book is intended to provide accurate and authoritative information on the subject matter with the understanding that the use of the information is to be used at the reader's discretion. The author and publisher specifically disclaim any and all liability arising directly or indirectly from the use of any information contained in the book. If professional advice or other expert assistance is required, the service of an appropriate and competent professional should be found.

Dedication

To Our Furred Friends:

This book was written in an effort to heal rifts between animals and their masters. I hope it will save "problem animals" from abuse and abandonment, by alleviating stress in both. My "human" book, Be Your Own Therapist, was my contribution to the emotional well being of readers by giving them the tools to change their lives on their own. Be Your Own Pet Therapist is my effort to do the same for our best friends, with the help of their owners and handlers. The step by step instruction, found within, is easy to learn and fun to do. If you can follow a recipe you can Be Your Own Pet Therapist.

"In life, be the type of person your pet thinks you are"

Anonymous

Bluey

"Be sure to have your pet spayed or neutered" – Bob Barker

Contents

Forward

If you picked up this book, you probably own a dog, cat, horse or other domestic pet. You may be a veterinarian or engaged in other occupations that bring you into close contact with animals. Even though you love your pet, you may find certain behaviors unacceptable. Perhaps your pet is skittish, afraid of strangers or loud noises, barks too much, pees when excited, or is too aggressive. These are symptoms of stress. Stress is becoming endemic in our society. We are besieged by demands on our time and patience and the pressure trickles down...from family members to household pets. As a result, increasing numbers of animals are simply abandoned, sent to shelters, by those no longer willing to care for them, and/or are mistreated by unhappy pet owners. Millions of pet owners and handlers, who may be experiencing these and related problems, don't know how to solve them.

The answer lies in new discoveries in energy psychology which have revolutionized the field and provided easy and humane solutions to behavior problems in animals (and humans). I have been using what I call Rapid Response (energy) Therapy (RRT) for many years in my practice, teaching seminars, conferences and writing many books and papers on the subject.[1] I have also raised, owned and shown both dogs and cats a good part of my life. From my study of the energy system, I know that animal bodies and brains function very like our own. Animals produce natural substances like, opiates, prostaglandins, adrenaline, nor-adrenaline and corticosteroids, associated with physical and psychological stress, in the same way that we do. Like us, animals have energy systems, and like us, they can benefit from new discoveries in treating stress. Human adults and children can access past traumas and other negative energetic experiences simply by thinking about them. Infants and animals cannot. Like infants, animals can only bring about a negative reaction or fear when actualy facing one. For this reason, both can only be treated at the time the stressful incident is happening. I reasoned that if one could successfully treat infants, as I have, why not animals? As I imagined it would, the process works the same way.

Because of the demand, a growing number of people offer all kinds of solutions for problem animals, i.e., pet psychics, trainers, 'horse whisperers' and the like. RRT is a more effective, rapid and low cost alternative. We need help in understanding and raising our pets. Since animals cannot treat themselves, they need you, the owner, to provide the solution. Using Rapid Response Therapy (RRT) with our furry friends is compassionate, and extends our understanding of how, like us, animals really are. In return they serve us in many ways. Therapy dogs, cats (and even miniature horses), are used to soothe and help heal, the aged, children, and others, who respond positively to their soft and insistent presence. Dogs provide eyes for the blind. Most of all they are our most loyal companions. When there are problems we must solve them together.

Susan Wright, Ph.D.

Chapter 1

Tale of a Puppy with a Severe Behavior Problem

If I knew then what I know now about Rapid Response Therapy, the following experience with a new puppy might have changed the outcome for both of us.

When I was a junior at Cornell University, I desperately wanted a pet. We, (my new husband and I) decided to visit the only pet store in Ithaca, N.Y., where the university is located. At the store, the owner showed us photographs of a litter of five ready-to-be-sold puppies…fantastic looking animals called Afghan Hounds. She lived in a forested area of Ithaca, where these magnificent animals had plenty of freedom to roam. Ithaca is a city of trees and there happened to be an entrance to the forest, just behind our rented house.

Eager to visit the puppies, we went to her home. Four of the five pups ran up to us immediately. One stayed back. It was clear to this budding therapist-to-be, that he was "special". For me he was a green light. My husband wasn't so sure. The owner was well known in the community, so I was confident the pup had not been mistreated. On the other hand, I was certain that I could "cure" him with love and attention. With my help, he was going to grow up to be friendly and outgoing. Wrong! He ran away every time anyone so much as approached the house, and he wouldn't return for hours. Catching him was out of the question. Over uneven ground, Afghan Hounds are faster than greyhounds. If trapped inside the house and a stranger (to him) was admitted, he would make himself unbelievably small, in an effort to disappear, and hide, head first, under the couch. His behavior named him. I called him BOO"! Because I loved BOO, eventually, I had to admit defeat and return him to the seller, where he would be free to roam with others. Heart broken, I had learned my lesson. Eventually, time passed and a new litter became available. This time I chose the boldest puppy.

I understand now that BOO had a phobia. Phobic tendencies

are hereditary in both humans and animals and can be healed (often in minutes) using energy therapy.[1] [2] The large numbers of patients, conference attendees, and seminar students, plus readers of my book (on humans), *Be Your Own Therapist,* who have been healed by RRT, are a testament to the effectiveness of the therapy.

REVIEW

The thought that perhaps animals could be treated, using the same energy based techniques I was using on human subjects, occurred to me because of a personal experience I had with a pet, earlier in my life. Later, the study of energy based therapy and Neurolinguistic Programming, led me to an understanding, that since (we) animals are all related, I could see no reason why RRT wouldn't work on both.

Chapter 2

What Is Rapid Response Therapy?

In order to understand how and why energy therapy works with animals, we must begin with human subjects. I had been a therapist for over 25 years when I discovered a strange advertisement on the back of a psychology magazine. It was for something called Thought Field Therapy, developed by a Dr. Roger Callahan. This was purportedly a process which did not use talk therapy or behavior modification to alleviate emotional problems -- instead, the therapy was based on the way energy flows throughout the body. It was not solely based upon the brain or cognition, but on body/mind responses to stress. [1] I found this whole approach difficult to believe but it immediately caught my interest. I was familiar with acupuncture and knew a bit about the import of the human energy system. I was both fascinated enough to explore the possibilities, and, at the same time, skeptical about the outcome. Intrigued, I sent for some material.

Thought Field Therapy was not only a radical departure from both traditional and nontraditional therapies but flew in the face of most of what I had learned about treating people. Based upon using Nature's own vital body/mind energy system, it claimed to be able to alleviate, even cure, common psychological problems. That was all very well and good. But would it really work? I decided to experiment on myself first. No harm done there. It not only worked but, as advertised, it worked fast, often in minutes! Using myself as the guinea pig, I tried several different treatments and noted that they were not only effective but that there was no exceptional discomfort involved. Reopening old emotional wounds can be painful, which is why professionals often tell patients that "things may get worse before they get better." Since my experience with this new form of treatment was so painless and effective, I decided to move ahead and talk to some of my clients about this mystery treatment, give them information for decision-making, and ask if they would like to try it. The treatment modality I decided to use first was the phobia technique. I knew from experience, how difficult phobias were to eliminate. (Some clinical professionals claim that it can't be done.) [2] It was so effective that I eventually enrolled in Dr. Callahan's training programs. Over time, I was certified to teach at the most advanced levels.

After years of exploring, using, adding to and refining the techniques, I wanted to introduce energy therapy in a simplified form that the general public could use on their own initiative. I called the technique Rapid Response Therapy (RRT) because that is what it is. By this time, I had discovered that the technique was totally safe and that there were no adverse reactions, which, in itself, set it apart from more traditional psychological treatment. Obviously there were many other differences (listed below):

- RRT is easy to learn.
- It is based upon the energy system.
- No reliving of the past

- There are no, cultural, age, sex, language or other barriers because RRT is not language based.

- It is very rapid (works often in minutes).

- It is cost effective and affordable

- It treats 30 common emotional problems in a completely different way.

- It is totally safe.

- RRT bypasses cognition and behavior.

- You can now learn to do it on yourself

In the fall of 2003, the book I had written to teach others how to use RRT on themselves, *Be Your Own Therapist,* was published. It served a two-fold purpose (1) to teach members of the public how to heal themselves and (2) to include more complex instructions for health professionals to use when working with clients. The book was the inspiration for treating our furry friends.

REVIEW

Dr. Roger Callahan took a giant leap forward and discovered a way to use the energy system to alleviate psychological problems. Prior to this discovery, energy practitioners focused on physical problems. Thought Field Therapy and its offshoot, Rapid Response Therapy, bypass both cognitive and behavioral traditional approaches to psychotherapy. They offer instead, direct access to the energy system. In contrast to more familiar treatment, RRT is rapid and safe. I believed the next step might be to try using the technique on animals.

Chapter 3

How Does Energy Therapy Work?

Energy is all around us. Right now, I am sitting in my office, writing this book, surrounded by radio, television, computer, and my own energy waves. I cannot see these waves, but they are there. In order to access this unseen electrical energy I must turn on a related switch. I must "tune in" the radio, computer or the television, if I want to use them. Our bodies are also electric. In order to bring negative energy (stress) into the body/mind where we can treat it, we must also tune in. We do this by thinking about the problem, bringing all the sensory information (visual, auditory and feeling related to the event), into focus, flooding our bodies with our stress reaction to it. We call this human energy switch the thought field. [1]

How does simply thinking about something make

memories and/or imaginary events real to us? It is the nature of the mind/body/spirit organism. The brain is a hard drive, or storehouse for intense experiences, which are called imprints. Events perceived as significant and/or important to our survival, are stored for future reference. Negative (and/or positive) imprints, formed during childhood, can become fixed and are reactions repeated as we mature. We can become trapped in fixed childlike responses to adult situations and, in the case of negative reactions, to a life of repeating mistakes. Even though our motives may be to overcome these mistakes by entering in to similar situations, in effect reliving them, hoping that this time they will turn out different, unfortunately, we have already been programmed to choose a similar cast of characters and outcome. These early imprints limit our ability to use all our resources. [2]

The brain doesn't know the difference between what we imagine (think about) and what is real. Haven't you ever had a nightmare? The events in the dream are not actually happening, are they? But they seem real to us and we react to them as though they are. Our senses go on alert. These information gathering senses are the mind's software (see, hear, feel, smell, touch) and are the brain's only source of information. The brain and the body are not separate entities. Eastern cultures have known for centuries that the mind does not operate independently from the body. Here, in the west, we are just now waking up to the fact. Originally focused on the organ pathways (meridians) of the body in order to heal *physical* problems (acupuncture and applied kinesiology), we have recently discovered that accessing energy meridians, by tapping on them, works just as well to alleviate *emotional* responses. [3]

Practitioners of RRT do not use needles. Instead, we use the fingers to tap on the energy meridians of the body/mind, in a selected sequence, defined by the problem being addressed. The treatment is based on this new understanding of how the body/mind/spirit system works on an emotional level....a kind of energy stimulus/response mechanism. The energy system is electrical. Our bodies are receivers. In order to access negative energy, associated with a problem, we must first think about the problem. When we do this, we bring in all the sensory input that goes with it. [4] This thought field is the doorway... the switch. The recipe or structure of the RRT process goes like this: [5]

- Choose the type of problem you want to change
- Think about the problem you want to alleviate. Visualize it, think what you say to yourself when it is happening, and then allow the feeling to flood your body, bringing the negative energy impulses into your body/mind system.
- Now, rate the intensity of stress you are feeling on a 10-1 stress scale, 10 equals intense discomfort and 1-0, an absence of stress. This is your measurement tool. As you do the treatment, decreasing numbers indicate lessening of negative responses.
- Look up the problem you want to treat and follow the energy tapping directions. At certain intervals you will re-evaluate your stress level.
- An absence of stress (0-1) scale means that you can

no longer react to the problem you are treating. It does not erase the memory, it only eliminates the stress associated with it. [6]

REVIEW

The mind is not localized in the brain which is only a small part of the puzzle. The mind permeates the body and beyond. The lessons, learned in childhood and stored in the brain, can come back to haunt us. We have found that the energy source accessed by RRT is, like the mind, a phenomenon that treats the mind and body as a unit. Against this new information, we can understand that the brain is a hard-wired storage house for past experiences, accessed through the sensory systems and stored as memories, through the activity of hormones and neurons, that is, the patterns of electrical connections of the brain and the reactions of the body. We can transform these connections by means of the RRT process.

Chapter 4

Why and How RRT Works With Animals

In my best selling book, *Be Your Own Therapist,* and in related seminars and speaking events, I teach others how to use the energy system to heal themselves. I lay out easy to learn, rapid, specific recipes, for alleviating 30 common emotional problems. The basic structure of the treatment is always the same, only the recipes for the specific problems are different. Rapid Response Therapy is done in easily learned steps. If you can follow a recipe, you can treat yourself, and now…. your pet.

Treating pets comes from our experience with treating infants. Infants are not capable of thinking about a problem on demand. Instead, they must be treated while they are experiencing stress. The following is a cogent description of how the treatment works on infants:

In March 2004, after presenting Rapid Response Therapy at the First Pacific Rim Energy Conference in Singapore, I boarded a Singapore Airlines 16 hour flight home. The huge airliner was filled to capacity. There were several families with infants, waiting in the boarding area. One family, in particular, caught my eye…an Indian family playing with an adorable, laughing little boy. I had requested a bulkhead seat so that I could stretch out my legs and, maybe, fall asleep during the flight back to San Francisco, totally unaware that, during long flights, the bulkhead was used to hang portable baby beds. As a result, I later found myself surrounded by infants. On board, the Indian family I had noticed earlier, took the two seats next to me. It was 9:30 P.M. and all the babies were tired and stressed. Of course, when the airplane took off and the pressure changed, the crying began. I expected that. However, when the plane leveled off, the cries simply accelerated. Mothers and fathers alternated walking their stressed babies up and down the aisles. Nothing worked. I decided to act. I turned to my seat mates and their screaming baby. I informed them that I believed I could help calm their infant. Of course, they didn't believe me. After years of teaching, I was used to that reaction. I explained that I had just come from Singapore, where I had been invited to teach a form of energy therapy that I was sure would work. At this point, they were willing to try anything and, so, I imagine, were the other passengers. Tapping on myself, I showed the couple how to do the simple anxiety algorithm (eye, arm, collarbone). Mirroring my tapping, they repeated the instructions on the baby. He stopped crying immediately and fell asleep in minutes. Put in his hanging bed, he slept for almost 12 hours. Another parent, across the isle, who had been watching the proceedings, asked me to show him "how to do that". The second infant, and then a third were treated with the same result. Mission accomplished. Peace restored.

Pet therapy follows a similar pattern. Like infants, animals cannot "think about a problem", they simply react. But we can still treat them. Animals have the same mind/ body connections as we do. Everything circulates through blood, lymph and energy systems, which communicate freely with the mind/body and with each other. Logically, healing touch and meridian tapping should relax and heal our pets in the same way it does humans.[1] Although pets have physical characteristics similar to our own, they cannot think about something simply by asking them to, so we must skip the thought process and go directly to the reactive phase, i.e., the situation which produced the stress in the first place. We can then proceed, using the same procedures on pets that we use on ourselves. The crucial difference is that treatment can only be effective *when the stress reaction is occurring or we have recreated it.*

Case Illustration

In my home we have two cats. One is a Scottish Fold (my cat), and the other, an Exotic (my son's cat). They are as different as day and night. Cappuccino, the Exotic, behaves like a dog. He is everyone's friend. Bluey, the Scottish Fold, is reticent. By nature, Scottish Folds are quiet, affectionate, and sleep a lot. Exotics, on the other hand are more outgoing. Not only are their breed characteristics different but so was their early experience. Cappuccino was bred in San Francisco. I simply had to drive him home. He was fine. At 10 weeks, Bluey was flown all the way from Florida, with stops in between. He was one traumatized kitten. He had such a hard time that I had to force feed him for two months. The result was that he bonded to me with a vengeance. I am mostly quiet and gentle with both cats. My son, an ardent animal lover, is more active, exuberant, and has a louder voice. He and Cappy play "catch me if you can". If he tries to play with Bluey, the cat takes off. I don't think Bluey is actually afraid of my son, instead, he is used to quiet, gentle me. To change this stress reaction, I decided to try to treat Bluey, using RRT. My solution was to have my son stand in the doorway, while I tapped on the proper meridians for stress. Then I asked him to move toward Bluey as I continued tapping. After repeating this process several times, it worked. Bluey will, most often, stay put when my son approaches. He even tolerates being picked up occasionally.

There is an alternative tapping technique which works with both infants and animals. *We treat the pet owner* (or the parent) instead of tapping directly on the pet. *The owner must be holding or touching the pet* as he/she uses the relevant tapping recipe on him/herself. I learned this approach during my training in Neurolinguistic Programming.[2] Energy fields intersect and there is a direct energy transfer from owner, to pet.

I know that all this is difficult to believe. Remember, I too was skeptical. It is out of the realm of our personal experience. We have a name for this reaction. We call it the Apex problem.[3] I am faced with this reaction during every seminar or speaking engagement. It is difficult for people to believe that something unfamiliar to them or that they have never experienced, will work. We have been conditioned to believe that we must *talk* about our problems, sometimes for months or years, in order to alleviate them. Energy therapy bypasses this belief. Instead, we treat the subject as soon as we can define the presenting problem. After that, we can choose the proper remedy. Despite the doubts, RRT definitely does work. Experiencing the treatment is proof enough. Nonetheless, even after the problem has been alleviated, I am often asked if it will *last*. The answer is yes.

Today the word of the effectiveness of RRT is spreading. I believe that, eventually, RRT will be included in treatment and training options used by veterinarians, animal trainers, pet handlers, and anyone else who is commonly brought into close contact with animals. It is my hope that, *Be Your Own Pet*

Therapist will spread the word to the general public so that animal lovers will become aware that RRT will heal animals.

REVIEW

After years of learning, writing about, and teaching Rapid Response Therapy to others and having them learn how to rapidly and easily heal themselves, it was natural for me to try the same tapping procedures on pets, beginning with my own. Adults can be asked to "think about the problem" they want to alleviate. Infants and animals cannot. Infants, animals must be treated only when a stressful situation is in progress and/or is being slowly introduced.

There is an alternative approach for very skittish animals. You can treat yourself, while holding your pet. Energy systems interact. The kind of treatment process we use is almost identical. (See chapter 10)

Chapter 5

Getting Started

In the following pages you will learn everything you need to know in order to easily treat your pet's fears and behaviors. The relaxation exercises and stress alleviation information recipes, listed in the text, include drawings, and photographs, to guide you through a step by step process. The time you take to learn these simple techniques will pay off by making your pet a loyal, happy addition to your family.

The following list of treatable symptoms covered in this book. [1]

STRESS SYMPTOMS	**BODY LANGUAGE**
Licking	Tail position
Fur stands up	Ear movements
Shaking	Eye contact
Crying	Erect/relaxed posture
Hiding	Other
Panting	

TYPES OF BEHAVIOR

STRESS SYMPTOMS	BODY LANGUAGE
Jumping	Compulsive, repetitive
Biting	Other aggressive behavior
Mounting	Lack of verbal responsiveness
Cowering	Submission/dominance
Excitement	Barking
Other	

Chapter 6

Relaxation Touching [1]

A wise first step in treating animals is to relax them and make them more aware of their bodies. It is not absolutely necessary to use the following exercises before treating your pet with RRT, but it will make the whole process easier and more fun. Touch influences animal learning at a cellular level just as it does with humans. Relaxing animals with touch is usually pleasurable to them. It teaches them where their body parts are. However, if you touch a spot your pet doesn't like or a place he/she is "ticklish," don't go there. Move on. Keep the initial sessions short as you learn what works best and what doesn't. Remember, you are both involved. Be gentle, treating your pet as you would like to be treated. You can do the exercises with your pet sitting, standing, or lying down, which ever is easier. There are, however, certain boundaries which must be established:

The Dont's

1. Do not stare directly in your furry friend's eyes

2. Do not use or hand or body positions that may be perceived as threatening, like leaning over your pet or suddenly raising your hand.

3. If your pet is aggressive, use a muzzle until you are certain it is safe not to.

4. Remember, puppies and kittens like to play and sometimes bite. Give them something to chew on (not your fingers) while you work with them.

5. Move slowly.

6. Do not go from one exercise to another until you and your pet have mastered the first.

7. Be sensitive as to how much of this your pet will tolerate. Don't push it. Your pet will let you know. A few short sessions will do. The animals love it and often beg for more.

Suppose the animal in question is nervous or very young and resists your touches? Or, your pet may be fine at first but try to get away as soon as you begin touching him. This can happen. If so, try using the back of your hand, rather than your fingers, or you may have to contain him gently in the beginning, so he cannot move away.[2] Check to see if you are applying too much pressure, holding your breath, or doing too many circles in one place, or, maybe you just need to slow down.

Exercise 1: Body touch circles:[3]

1. Support the animal's head with your hand. Beginning at the top of the head, *lightly* begin to make interlocking clockwise circles, and proceed down the spine to the tail (or lack of same). Rarely, animals may prefer counterclockwise motion, or feel less threatened, when you use the back of the hand, instead of the fingertips. My cats prefer a "massage," opening and partially closing my fingers as I gently move around different sections of their bodies. But then cats like to be different. Try the rotating motion first

and use alternatives only when necessary. Let your pet be your guide.

2. Supporting the head, begin at the shoulder area, making circles on one side, just beneath the spinal area, back and forth until you have covered first one side and then the other.

Drawing:1

complete map of relaxation touch circles

Photo 1: *back circles*

Photo 2: *circles down the side*

Do not go on to next exercise until your pet is comfortable with the prior exercise.

Exercise 2: Tail pull

Run the tail through your hand from bottom to top, tugging gently at the end.

Photo 3: *tail pull*

Exercise 3: Ear touch.

Now, if your pet agrees, hold the ear between your fingers and make a few circles with your fingers, and then, holding the ear gently between the fingers, slip the ear between the fingers and on up to the tip. Do this on both ears. You will find that this often helps with ear cleaning.

Photo 4: *ear touch*

Exercise 4: Mouth touch.

If there is no resistance, holding your pet's head in your hand, make small, very gentle, circles on the muzzle, beginning at the nose, and moving upward towards the eye. Do both sides. If the animal is small, you may be able to do this with one hand. If your pet easily accepts this touch, you may be able to run your fingers along the teeth, under the lips. This exercise is calming to fearful animals, and makes brushing teeth easier. Animals need dental care and this technique can avoid later veterinarian bills.

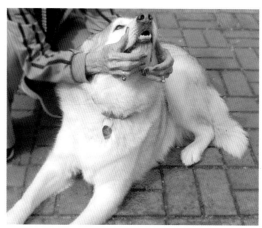

Photo 5: *mouth touch*

Exercise 5: Leg Touch.

Use two hands (one on each side of the leg for large dogs) or, if animal is small, you can simply wrap your whole hand around its leg. Begin where the upper leg meets the body and, slowly and gently, run your hands down to the beginning of the paw (where the ankle is on a human). Each leg is done separately.

Photo 6: *leg touch*

Exercise 6: Paw circles.

Gently take a paw in your hand and make gentle circles with your fingers. Separate the toes. This exercise helps with nail cutting.

Photo 7: *paw circles*

REVIEW

Relaxing your pet before treatment is a good first step. It establishes a bond, calms both of you, and makes the animal more aware of its body parts. I find learning to relax your pet is a good idea, even if you never need to treat him energetically. It's a form of educated petting or stroking which promotes trust and has a positive effect. On the other hand, you can simply treat the behavior problem without this preparation.

Chapter 7

Treating Your Pet

Human tapping points were developed by Roger Callahan, Ph.D. and the animal points were derived from work with human subjects.[1] All tapping on animals can be done with the animal standing, sitting, or lying down, depending on which part you are accessing at the moment and the flexibility of the animal (some puppies and cats are like butter.) There are two ways to treat your pet (1) by tapping on the animal and (2) tapping on yourself while holding or touching the animal (Chapter 10). Tapping directly on your pet is the most common. When we use energy tapping on animals, we use the same alarm points (energy meridians) we use on people, with the exception of three locations which are anatomically different.[2] The following three animal physiology points are the exceptions:

1. Under the arm in human subjects (ua) is done on the side opposite the nipple area. (below) On animals, it is done on the side of the body (sb) adjacent to the leg. (next page)

Photo 8: *under arm human tapping point (ua)*

Photo 9: *side of the body (sb)*

2. All animal treatment points are tapped *gently but firmly* five times, *except one*, the energy reversal point. This point is *tapped 15 times on animals*. On humans, the reversal point is on the side of the hand between the little finger and the thumb (er). (below) On animals we tap on the side of the paw (er). (next page)

Photo 10: *Human Reversal Hand Point*

Photo 11: *Animal Energy Reversal Paw Point*

Repeat the treatment sequence several times. What you are looking for is a change in behavior. If there is little or no change it simply means that the energy system is *reversed,* or stuck, and has to be unstuck before the energy will flow freely. This also happens in treating humans. The treatment will not work until the block is removed.[2] You do this by tapping *15 **times*** on the side of the paw. Once the energy reversal is removed the treatment works perfectly. *Remember, it is necessary to do reversal tapping, once you have done the treatment sequence twice and there has been little or no positive change.* When you have removed the reversal, go back to the beginning of the treatment model and start over.

REVIEW

Treating animals is very similar to treating humans. There are, however, anatomical differences which must be taken into account. Human under arm, reversal point and gamut points are different. Under arm tapping is done on the animal's body, adjacent to the upper leg. The reversal point is on the side of the paw. The gamut point has no corresponding animal point, and so the process must be done on the person treating the pet, while in constant contact with the pet's body (see following chapter).

Chapter 8

The Nine Gamut (9g) [1]

There is another point called the gamut point which often is used as part of the treatment in animals. The gamut point is non existent in animals. In humans, the gamut point is located between the knuckle of the little finger and ring finger. It is always done on the pet owner while he/she is touching the pet. (see below)

Photo 12: *The Human Gamut Point*

On humans the 9gamut has a total of nine parts. The gamut is used to refine the treatment by informing the brain. The eyes are the windows of the soul. The 9gamut includes six eye movements, two humming sounds (right brain) and one counting (left brain) and is *always* used *between* identical treatment sequences. [1] This is important to know because, in certain circumstances, you may choose to do the entire treatment process on yourself, while holding your pet. (See Chapter 10). However**, there are conflicting opinions on whether or not it is necessary to do the 9gamut when treating animal subjects**. Like us, animals have energy systems, and like us, they can benefit from new discoveries in treating stress. We know that energy fields intersect. The theory is that when we tap on ourselves the effect is transferred to the animal. I know for a fact that this transference happens when treating infants. I use it on animals also, but the jury is still out. I suggest you try it both ways: *with* and *without*. Experience with energy therapy eventually led us to discard steps we believed at first to be essential. Animals cannot tell us if the treatment will work as well without the 9gamut. Results will. If you decide to include the 9gamut, you must follow the human model (treatment, 9gamut, repeat treatment.). The difference is that you tap, using the treatment of choice, *on your* **pet** and immediately follow it by doing the 9gamut *on yourself,* while *remaining in physical contact anywhere on the body of the animal,* and then repeated the selected treatment sequence on the animal. In other words, you do the 9gamut *for* them, since animals have neither a gamut point nor the ability to follow the directions.

Treatment model including the 9gamut

1. Choose indicated treatment:

2. Do treatment sequence on your pet

3. Do the following steps, while in physical contact with your pet. Tapping continually on the gamut spot (between the knuckle of the middle and little finger). (See following page, **Photo 13**)

Photo 13: *Doing the 9gamut while treating your pet*

Continue tapping and do the following:

- Open your eyes
- Close your eyes
- Move your eyes down right
- Move your eyes down left
- Roll your eyes around in one direction
- Roll them in the opposite direction
- Hum a few bars of a tune aloud
- Count to five aloud
- Repeat humming

4. Repeat the identical treatment sequence on your pet.

If, after several applications, there isn't a real reduction in the problem, use the animal reversal point (side of paw/hoof), tapping 15 times, and return to number 1. If the negative behavior should recur, repeat the treatment. Eventually the problem will dissipate.

Treatment model omitting the 9gamut:

1. Choose the animal treatment sequence that fits the problem

2. Administer treatment to pet

3. Repeat identical treatment sequence, twice. If there isn't a real reduction in the problem, use the animal reversal point (side of paw) and return to number 1.

REVIEW

The 9gamut has always been an integral part of the treatment process in human subjects. I use it with animals, but its value may be overstated. Over time, there have been other, once essential, parts of energy treatment which have been found to be unnecessary to a successful outcome, specifically, affirmations and the muscle test, making it possible to simplify the process so that individuals can use the treatment recipes on themselves. However, it would be wise to include it in the beginning.

Chapter 9

Location of All Animal Treatment Points

We begin with an animal drawing of all the tapping points and their locations.[1]

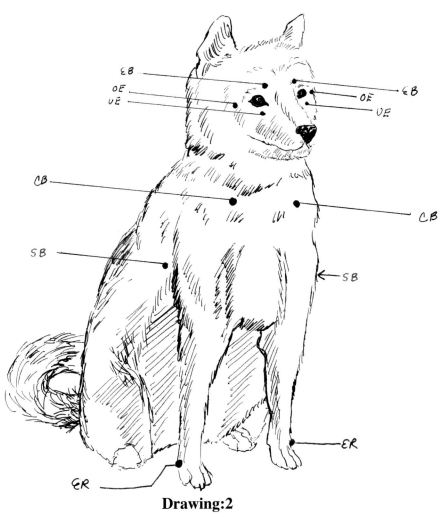

Drawing:2

animal drawing showing all points used in treatment

53

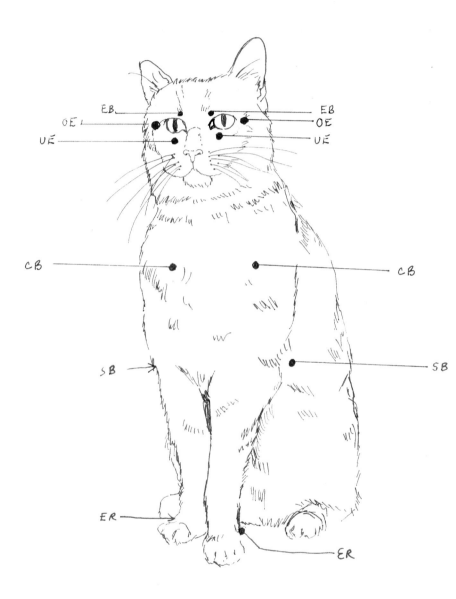

EB

OE

UE

EB

OE

UE

CB

CB

SB

SB

ER

ER

54

Photo 14

Under eye (ue): Just under mid point of eye

Photo 15

Eyebrow (eb): Point just above the eye next to the nose

Photo 16

Outside of eye (oe): Above and just outside the corner of the eyebrow toward the ear.

Photo 17

Side of body (sb): Tap just between the top of the leg and the side of the animal

Photo 18

Collarbone (cb): Where the neck forms a V as it reaches the chest, move about a half inch down and one inch to either side.

9gamut: arbitrary. If simple recipe isn't sufficient, try inserting the 9g in the middle (tapping on yourself) then repeat tapping points on pet **(see Chapter Seven: photo 13)**

Energy Reversal (er): When behavior doesn't change after two repetitions of the tapping recipes, tap outside of paw or hoof. 15 times then go back to the beginning. Repeat as often as needed until behavior changes. **(See Chapter 7: Photo 11).**

REVIEW

The treatment recipe format is always the same. Look up the problem that you want to change, follow the directions and repeat treatment sequence. I personally use the 9gamut, on myself, in between two identical treatment recipes on my pet, but it may not be necessary to include this. Instead, you may want to try simply using the appropriate tapping problem resolution twice, omitting the 9gamut on yourself in between.

Chapter 10

Tapping Model for Specific Problems

Treatment Outline:

- Treat your animal while in the perceptual field.

- Position human and animal subject.

- Choose the appropriate treatment recipe.

- Tap each point in sequence five times.

- Repeat identical treatment recipe.

- If no behavior change, administer energy reversal

  tapping.

- Go back to the beginning and repeat.

- Observe behavior

TYPE OF PROBLEM	TAPPING SEQUENCES
Phobias and fears	Tap 5 times each: under eye: (side of body near upper leg) collarbone, 9gamut, repeat sequence.
Anxiety	The same treatment as phobias and fears (above)
Claustrophobia	Tap 5 times each: side of body, (near upper leg), under eye, collarbone, 9gamut, repeat sequence.
Trauma	Tap five times each: eye-brow, under eye, side of body, collarbone, 9gamut, repeat sequence.
Obsessive behavior	Tap five times on each: col-larbone, under eye, collarbone, 9gamut, repeat sequence.
Aggression	Tap five times each: under eye, side of body, collarbone, outside of eye, collarbone, 9gamut, repeat sequence.

Energy Reversal	Side of paw/hoof, 15 times and repeat if the behavior doesn't change, after doing the treatment twice.
Pain	Experimental algorithm. This is only a temporary measure to alleviate pain. Keep your hand in contact with your pet, in close proximity to the pain area. Tap 50 times on your gamut point, five times on pet's collarbone, then do 9gamut exercise and repeat sequence. Do this several times. If persistent, do reversal and repeat. It may help.

See illustrations of cat and dog on pages 30 and 31

Chapter 11

Surrogate Tapping Method

It may be that you have an extremely frightened or shy animal that must be held. If so, holding the animal on your lap or under one arm, it is still possible to do the treatment. However, you must treat yourself as a surrogate for your pet. Energy fields interact. The tapping energy will transfer to your pet.[1] Maintaining constant body contact with your pet, tap on yourself, using instead the related points for human subjects, i.e., tapping on the human equivalents for animals points, most of which are identical. On the opposite page, you will find a drawing of a human subject with the comparable meridian tapping points.[2]

LOCATION OF TAPPING POINTS ON HUMAN SUBJECTS

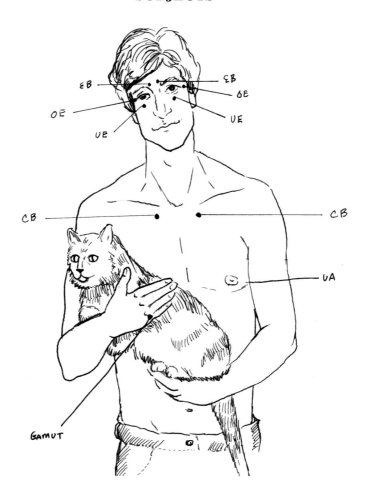

- **Under eye (ue):** **(same as animal treatment point)**

- **Eyebrow (eb): (Same as in animals)**

- **Outside of eye (oe):** **(Same as in animals)**

- **Under arm (ua):** This point is different. Tap under your arm, opposite the nipple area.

- **Collarbone (cb):** Pretty much the same for human or animal subject. Tap where the neck forms a V as it reaches the chest, move down an inch and one inch to either side.

- **Gamut (9g)**

- **Energy Reversal (er):** Side of hand, 5 times. Repeat as often as needed. Remember to do the treatment, the gamut, followed by the identical treatment. Do this several times. If results are poor, tap on reversal point (side of hand between little finger and wrist), five times, and repeat the sequence, **(treatment, 9gamut, treatment.)**

When I treat myself while holding a pet, following the human equivalent directions for pet anxiety treatment (under eye, under arm, collarbone, 9gamut, repeat sequence), I play an imaginary game. I imagine a time when I felt anxious myself and rate the intensity on a scale of 10-1 before I tap on the animal. Ten is high anxiety and so on down the scale. While holding my pet, I do one entire sequence (under eye, under arm, collarbone, 9gamut, repeat.), while thinking about the problem. (Sometimes, I imagine how my pet is feeling). Then I do the gamut, and re-peat the treatment. I check my pet to see if there has been improvement. If not, I tap on my reversal point and go back to the beginning.

REVIEW

There is an alternative way to treat oversensitive animals. You do it by tapping on yourself, while holding the pet, and doing the human equivalent treatment format for the problem at hand. The form of treatment is identical to the instructions for animals. However, you use your own body and human tapping points not found on animals. I sometimes like to imagine I am feeling a similar kind of stress, while using this method or, perhaps, imagine how my pet feels.

Chapter 12

It Is Your Turn Now

We are entering a new era where tradition and holistic medicine are beginning to overlap. Ancient treatments for disease and the use of medicinal plants are being rediscovered. Although it is difficult to change fixed ideas and beliefs (scientific and otherwise) we are approaching a period of new discovery and a change in the philosophical climate. Resistance is still strong, but it is becoming more difficult to refute the efficacy of a treatment, when you can see it working with your own eyes.

Now that you have had personal experience understanding how the energy system can be used to heal animals, why not heal yourself? Having already worked with your pet will make working with yourself a breeze. The important point is that there is no risk or harm involved for either of you. Tapping on humans to alleviate emotional stress is a revolutionary advance in psychotherapy and counseling, and the process in treating yourself is similar to the treatment you have already used in changing the negative behavior of your pet. The major difference between them is the number of problems involved. On the other hand, in some ways, it is both easier and quicker for us to treat ourselves, since we are capable of recreating a trauma or stress related problem simply by *thinking about it*, while animals and infants cannot. When treating animals or infants, we must either wait until the problem arises or do something to recreate it. All we need to do in alleviating our own problems is to recall the troublesome events. Just by thinking about them, we trigger all the sense related information (mental software) ,i.e., seeing, hearing, feeling, and even smelling and tasting (both powerful memory inducers) stored in our memory banks. (I never think about my wonderful grandmother without remembering her particular smell and the related smells and tastes associated with cooking chocolate fudge at her home.) The candy never came out right but it tasted great. I will probably die trying to get it to harden properly.

Treating human subjects is somewhat more complex

than treating animals, but that should come as no surprise. Even though we share similar physiology, human mind/body connections are far more complex. We are "thinking" animals and capable of all creating all sorts of problems. Nonetheless, RRT renders even our more sophisticated makeup easier to remedy than more traditional treatment methods.

Because RRT is so different from traditional therapies it amazes and confuses participants. Even after a successful treatment, the participant may have trouble accepting the treatment of the energy system and tapping on meridians as responsible for the outcome. Instead he/she may credit "being distracted" or even, "I guess I didn't really have the problem in the first place". Of course, since they are focusing on the problem throughout the entire process, distraction is not a valid argument. Once the treatment is over, the problem stays gone. It is just hard to reject what we have been taught to expect.

For those readers interested in trying RRT on themselves, you can buy my recent, popular book, *Be Your Own Therapist*...the forerunner to and the inspiration for *Be*

Your Own Pet Therapist. In it you will find similar instructions for healing the following common emotional problems.

Traumas	Nasal congestion
Addictions	Stress
Obsessions	Clumsiness
Anger	Reversal of words,
Fatigue	negativity
Guilt	Jet lag
Depression	TMJ
Pain	Visualization
Embarrassment	Peak performance
Shame	Panic/Anxiety
Jealousy	Phobias
rage	
Inhalant type toxins	

The step by step process is easy to do. The history and science behind energy therapy is included in the book as are additional instructions for health professionals working with others.

In the back of the book you will find information on how and where to order.

Chapter 13

Closing Remarks

Because I love animals, it was natural for me to wonder about using RRT to treat them. At this time there are few therapists actively involved in using energy based therapy with our furred friends. It is important that there be more. We want to improve their lives. *Be Your Own Pet Therapist* is written to fill that void with the hope that more professional animal handlers, veterinarians, and pet owners will become aware of the benefits of this type of treatment.

Therapy based upon the energy system is still in its infancy. Research on the efficacy of using the energy system to treat a myriad of problems is continuing. As to its future, we are just scratching the surface

I hope you and your pet will benefit from the advice contained in these pages. Once you get the knack of following the treatment recipes, it is quite easy. I believe it will give you a sense of accomplishment and control without having to resort to punishment. Instead, be sure to include copious praise and an occasional treat and I guarantee your pet will respond enthusiastically to all the encouragement you give. Remember, they will love you no matter what. Return the favor.

REFERENCES

FORWARD
1. Wright, Susan Ph.D., *Be Your Own Therapist,* Mill Valley, CA, Vision Books International, Publisher, 2003, pp. 2-9.

CHAPTER 1
1. Wright, Susan Ph.D., *Be Your Own Therapist,* Mill Valley, CA, Vision Books International, Publisher, 2003, pp. 12-14.
2. Durlacher, James, Dr., *Freedom From Fear Forever,* Tempe, Arizona, Van Ness Publisher, 1995, pp. 97-104.

CHAPTER 2
1. Wright, Susan Ph.D., *Be Your Own Therapist,* Mill Valley, CA, Vision Books International, Publisher, 2003, pp. xvii-xx.
2. Adler, Tina, *Studies Look At Ways To Keep Fear At Bay,* APA Monitor Magazine, Toronto, Canada, November 11, 1993

CHAPTER 3
1. Harmon, Willis, *Global Mind Change*, San Francisco, CA, Barrett-Koehler, Publisher, 1998, p. 69.
2 Wright, Susan Ph.D., *Be Your Own Therapist,* Mill Valley, CA, Vision Books International, Publisher, 2003. pp.4-6 and pp.18-22
3. Ibid. pp. 41-42
4. Bandler, Richard & MacDonald, Will, *An Insider's Guide To Submodalities,* Cupertino, CA., Meta Publishers, 1988, p. 8
5. Wright, Susan Ph.D., *Be Your Own Therapist,* Mill Valley, CA, Vision Books International, Publisher, 2003, pp. 75-79.
6. Wright, Susan Ph.D., *Be Your Own Therapist,* Mill Valley, CA, Vision Books International, Publisher, 2003, p. 40.

CHAPTER 4
1. Wright, Susan Ph.D., *Be Your Own Therapist,* Mill Valley, CA, Vision Books International, Publisher, 2003, p 3.
2. NLP Health Certification Training, Salt Lake City, February, 7, 1996
3. Wright, Susan Ph.D., *Be Your Own Therapist,* Mill Valley, CA, Vision Books International, Publisher, pp. 226-229.

CHAPTER 5
1. Danzig, Victoria, LCSW, TFTdx, *TFT With Animals, A Cross-Species Experience,* Presentatiion at the First Annual Conference for Thought Field Therapy, Hilton San Diego Airport/Harbor Island, San Diego, CA., October 26-27. 2002.

CHAPTER 6
1. Tellington-Jones, Linda, *Getting In T Touch With Your Dog,* North Pomfret, VT., Trafalgar Square Publishing, 2001, pp. 12-14.
2. Ibid. p. 27
3. Ibid. pp. 26-38

CHAPTER 7
1. Callahan, Roger, Ph.D., TFT™ Training, Indian Wells, CA., November 2, 1997 & Wright, Susan Ph.D., *Be Your Own Therapist,* Mill Valley, CA, Vision Books International Publisher, 2003, Chapter 6. This information is included in Dr. Callahan's publications and books. It has been reprinted, enhanced, by Fred

Gallo, James Durlacher, and many others in related books.

2. Zidonis and Snow, *The Accu Cat, a guide to Feline Acupressure* & *The Well Connected Dog, a guide to Canine Acupressure,* Larkspur, CO, Tallgrass Publishers, LLC. Good additional reference.

CHAPTER 8

1. Callahan, Roger, Ph.D., TFT™ Training, Indian Wells, CA., November 2, 1997

2. Zidonis and Snow, *The Accu Cat, a guide to Feline Acupressure* & *The Well Connected Dog, a guide to Canine Acupressure,* Larkspur, CO, Tallgrass Publishers, LLC.

CHAPTER 9

1. Zidonis and Snow, *The Accu Cat, a guide to Feline Acupressure* & *The Well Connected Dog, a guide to Canine Acupressure,* Larkspur, CO, Tallgrass Publishers, LLC

1. NLP Health Certification Training, Salt Lake City, February, 7, 1996

2. Callahan, Roger, Ph.D., TFT™ Training, Indian Wells, CA. October 3-November 1997.

CHAPTER 10

1. Eden, Donna, with Feinstein, David, *Energy Medicine, N.Y., N.Y.,* Penguin/Putnam Publishers, 1999, pp. 55-56

2. Callahan, Roger, Ph.D., TFT™ Training, Indian Wells, CA. November 2, 1997

To order books and products written by Dr.Wright:
Go to Dr. Wright's website:
www.creativelifechangebooks.com
or
www.advicelink.com
Or you can go to your nearest bookstore or Amazon.com
To contact Dr. Wright directly, call (toll free) 800 Linkage
1 (800) 546-5243